Team Building Activities

Team Building Activities - Create A Winning Team With 30 Team Building Activities

Get Our Free Book
50 Productivity Ideas

Get the book here:

mindplans.com/free-productivity-book

Introduction

I want to thank you and congratulate you for downloading the book, *"Team Building Activities - Team Building Activities - Create A Winning Team With 30 Team Building Activities*

This book contains proven steps and strategies on how to organize team games, manage team activities, and get better results for your team building.

Team building is essential for building up a highly effective teams that not only work, but positively impact the company. Team games that cultivate teamwork not only highlight their individual strengths, but reveal their weaknesses. Team building activities that are well-planned end up showing each member's reliance on one another, creating that bond that will propel the entire team forward.

In this book you will learn what it takes to make the best team build activities, and team games, and how to make them progressive so your members will continuously learn and grow!

You will also read about common problems that may arise and things you should avoid. For a team building activity to be successful, it has to be hassle-free and problem-free. So, seeing the pitfalls beforehand will definitely ensure your team building will be fruitful.

Thanks again for downloading this book, I hope you enjoy it!

Table of Contents

Chapter 1
Team Building – Why It Is Necessary

Chapter 2
Team Building Games that Work

Chapter 3
Indoor Team Building Activities

Chapter 4
Outdoor Team Building Activities

Chapter 5
What to Watch Out For

Chapter 6

30 Team Building Games

Chapter 7

Evaluation of Results

Team Building – Why It Is Necessary

Chapter 1

If you've ever been in a team, you may have experienced team building activities at some point in your career. Some are fun, others physically challenging, but most are unforgettable. At first, you probably wondered what the activity was for. Most of the things you do in team building sessions have nothing to do with your actual job. Sometimes, your bosses just take you out to dinner, maybe do some karaoke. So, you think that perhaps team building is just a fancy acquaintance party.

However, if it was just a way to get to know each member of the team, why do it more than once? Also, there are some team building activities that are extremely physical—what are those meant to achieve? Are companies doing this to follow the work-life balance ideology?

The answer is simple: they want to cultivate harmony within the team.

Team building is actually an essential management tool. It is more than just getting to know each other or a reason to hang out. Team building has a purpose, and knowing what the activity is meant to do for you and your team will not only give more meaning to each experience, but will also improve your relationship with co-workers.

Sadly, there are many people, including leaders, who don't know the purpose of team building. So many of them will settle for common activities like dining or drinking, and while these are good as ice breakers, simple activities like these do not sufficiently cover the purpose of team building.

Now, before we start talking about team building activities, it is essential that a proper understanding of the word *team* is in place. What is a team? Well, a team is a group of people who work together, under one leadership, to achieve a common goal.

Think of the human body—the head is the leader and all the other body parts represent the members. Each part plays a role in coordination with the other parts, and the head—the brain—directs each of them towards the same goal. When one part goes to another direction, opposite to the rest of the parts of the body, harmony is lost and the goal will not be reached.

For example: Imagine your left foot insisting to go to the left direction when the rest of your body wants to go to the right. What will happen? You will be stuck where you are because you can't move. You need both feet to walk towards one direction only for you to move.

The same thing happens with a team. All the members play different roles and they will also have different strengths and weaknesses—each will need to compliment the other to form symmetry. The leader should be able to motivate his entire team to work for the same goals, and move towards the same direction.

However, getting people to work harmoniously as a team is not always a simple task. You are lucky if you get team members who automatically work harmoniously, and are willing and able to follow your direction. The normal scenario is that you get individuals who have different, and sometimes clashing, personalities. There will be members who will not only go against your leadership, but will create conflict within the group. You will also have individuals who have different plans in their careers, and might influence other members of the team.

You can't always choose the people you get to work with. More often than not, you will get brilliant people who don't work well together. Does that mean you give up on turning them into a unit? No. It is true that when a team doesn't work as a whole, it doesn't work at all, but that is where team building comes into play.

The objective of team building activities is to *unite* the team so that they work as a whole. Team building activities should aim to enhance the individual strengths of each member, while addressing their weaknesses, finding the perfect balance within the group. Where one person is weak, the other person will be strong, creating that symmetry that makes a team unbeatable. When the members work in harmony with each other, and with their leader, the team becomes invincible, and this is the goal and purpose of team building activities.

How do you know what kind of activities to do? The next chapter will tell you how.

Team Building Games that Work

Chapter 2

Planning team building activities should begin with the people the activity is meant for: the team. The leader should spend time with each member not only to assess their key performance metrics (their numbers), but their character, their personalities. Take note of how these personalities either compliment or clash with the other personalities, and then find out if the mix will work. Finding a common ground for each member will definitely be advantageous.

Then, look at all the work-related challenges the team is facing. Is it a problem with communication? Is it a problem with seniority? Is it a problem with the actual work, maybe some members are confused or conflicted with some of the duties? Is it a personal issue between members of the team? Learning some of the challenges preventing the team from working together harmoniously will make it easier to construct great team building activities.

So the idea is to spend time with each member, and assessing the team as whole. Make a checklist of all their strengths and weaknesses before formulating activities that will cater to those.

The next thing to do is the actual planning. First, a successful event will have the 4 C's: Commitment, Clarity, and Communication.

Commitment from each member to participate in the activities is essential. Clarity pertains to the understanding of each member. Is the objective of the activity clear to all the members of the team? Lastly, communication is the part of the activity where individual members are expected to define their role in the activity—what was in it for them? What was in it for the team? For the company as a whole? They should be able to communicate that properly after the event.

After all, the purpose is to create a well-oiled machine that works as a unit so that goals are met and the customer satisfied.

The next thing to consider is resources. You have to consider funds, venues, food, and materials needed. Also, if the activities will include travel, you need to consider transportation. Once everything is in order, then you can set a date.

After setting the date, make contingency plans for any untoward occurrences. For example, if the outdoor activity is cancelled due to weather conditions, there should be a backup activity indoors.

Once the details of the activities have been ironed out, it is time to tell the team. They have to be advised of proper decorum, which include right clothing and health status. If the activities require strenuous physical movements, make sure that everyone is fit enough to accomplish them.

Of course, you should also take into consideration the time the members have spent together as a team. If the team is new, perhaps activities that will get them acquainted with each other are necessary. If the members of the team are acquainted with each other, and the purpose of the activity is to build harmony, then focus on activities that will make them work together.

To make sure that team building is effective, the leaders must make sure that the members of the team will benefit from the event. So, it is best that competition is taken out of the exercises. The goal should always be to build the team.

Things to Avoid

Team building works on the same principle as competitive sports. If you are training for basketball, you need to practice a lot. If you only practice once a month, don't expect to win. Only continuous, regular training and exercise will give you any chance of winning.

The same thing with teams. An effective team building activity needs to be continuous, and progressive. In other words, it has to be part of the corporate culture.

So, avoid sporadic team building. Make it regular thing, which means a minimum of every three months, to a monthly event.

It is also a misconception to add competitiveness to team building activities. Again, you are not training to fight each other; the goal is to work together as a unit. So, remove all competition from your activities.

Indoor Team Building Activities

Chapter 3

There are many activities that can be done indoors for team building events, but listed below are the most popular ones. These have been divided according to purpose.

Getting to know

This activity is good for any group size; especially effective for new teams whose goal is to acquaint members of the team with each other. The "getting to know activity" should focus on the character of each member, and not their personal stories.

To do this, make charts for each member to write on. On the chart, right down several labels, and have them write their name under the label they think fits them. The labels should say, "Music Lover", "Has Kids", "Has been on TV", "Reads many books", etc.

Then, after they have written their names on the labels, tell them to exchange their paper with every other member until all the charts have been filled out by each member. Then, collect the charts, and in a separate chart, write down all the names that were written in each label.

Have each member say something about the answer they provided. Like if they wrote their name under "Music Lover", have them say something about the music they like, or if they wrote their name under "has kids", have them talk about their kids. Make notes on the answers they provide.

Who am I

This is an activity for a medium-sized group, and the idea is to remove the culture of stereotyping in your team. To do this activity:

Prepare nametags with 'personality types', and attach a name tag to each person's back. Of course, they are not supposed to see the tag on their backs, but they'll see everyone else's tag. Then, have each person go around to ask the other people clues about the personality type that is on his back. The questions should be stereotype-based like, "Am I a woman?" "Am I strong?" "Am I talented?" etc.

The other people, the ones being asked, can only say yes or no. So, the person asking the questions should keep asking until they have a good picture of the personality they have on their backs.

This activity will show how easy it is to stereotype a person based on their looks, work, talent, and character. So, it is information that they can either use to work harmoniously with, or learn from to better adapt.

If you need help with the kinds of personalities to write down, here are a few suggestions:

- Professor.

- Auto mechanic.

- Postal worker.
- Olympic medalist.
- Fast-food restaurant worker.
- Movie star.

Outdoor Team Building Activities

Chapter 4

Outdoor activities depend on the size of the venue and the number of participants. Below you will see a few suggestions based on the size of the team and the venue.

Put your faith in me

This activity's goal is to improve the trust each member has on each other. This works for small to medium sized teams, and requires a small to medium sized venue.

What you do is to have the members of the team line up from lightest to heaviest, and have them sit down on the ground. Have all the members raise their hands as if catching something in the air. Then the lightest person, who sits on the very front of the line, will stand and free-fall on his teammates. The members of the team will then catch him and move him using their hands and strengths back to the end of the line.

Do this until each member of the team has been able to ride the hands of their teammates. This is a strenuous physical activity that is both fun and scary—especially if the team has really big members—but if they are able to do this feat, the leader can use that as a motivational mantra, "You were able to carry him on your hands! This is nothing!"

This activity will not only develop trust among the team, but confidence in each individual member.

Walk me through the mines!

This is another fun activity to do outdoors, and one that you can use to remove friction among members who are already conflicted. Walk me through the mines forces them to work with each other in order to overcome obstacles.

So, what you do is prepare many mines—different sizes—for example, boxes, balls, and chairs. Pair the members into teams, and make sure to do strategic pairing, like pair a weak member with a strong one, or pair two people who have personality conflicts. This will promote teamwork between colleagues who, ordinarily, won't even sit together. Remember the object of the team games is to improve harmony.

The objective is to get to the other side without touching any of the mines. Blindfold one of the players, and this is the person who will go through the mines and should not say a word all throughout the activity. Then, the other player will be standing outside the mine field, giving instructions to the other person. If the blindfolded player hits a mine, he starts again.

Now, to make this even more effective, give each team time to talk about their strategy of communication five minutes before starting the activity. Once everyone's through, have them talk about the experience with the whole group.

Treasure hunt

This team building game will require some advanced scouring of the area. It is an actual treasure hunt where you will have a map, several meet up points in the venue, and obstacle courses that the members need to go through. This activity is good for large groups and for large venues, like a hiking trail or park.

The objective is to force the members to count on each other, harnessing quick thinking and reliability. They will only be given a map (of course, if this activity will be done at night, give them a flashlight as well). They will have to follow the map to get to meet up points where a new map will be given, and further instructions.

Each team will have a leader, which will be assigned by members of the team. There should be tasks that will test their intellect, their wit, their stamina, their strength, and their determination. For example, in one meet-up point, in order for them to get the next map and additional instructions for the next course of their trip, they have to solve a puzzle, or cross a bridge. These mini activities will give other members of the team a chance to show their skill. This highlights the different strengths of each member during all the activities.

At the end of the activity, have each one relate how they helped the team achieve the goal.

What to Watch Out For

Chapter 5

As with any activity, there will be some problems that you should watch out for. Of course, all these activities should be safe for everyone involved, or there should be plans to address any kind of emergency situation. However, there are other dangers that are not as obvious as say an injury or fire in the pantry.

Organizing events that will involve members of the team should have boundaries. Where do you draw the line on things? For example, if the event is a getting-to-know-you party, what's the control on alcohol? What about risqué behavior—what is your stand on that?

Below are some of the things you may want to watch out for during the event:

Legal issues

You have to make sure that there will be minimal to no legal issues before or after the activity. For example, a party that aims to acquaint members of the team may actually end up in accidents brought upon by alcohol. Some companies have actually decided not to include alcohol in company-related events, or to keep it at a minimum.

Impact on After-Work Life

Some of these activities might open doors that were already locked. For example, if the party will be an overnight event at a location, extra-marital affairs might ensue. What is the company's stand on romances among workmates? Remember, though it may not be right for the company to meddle in personal affairs, it is their duty to make sure that their employees are safe in these events. Part of safety should be looking at the possible risks and problems arising from such relationships.

Impact on Work-Related Performances

This is the reason why management should still get involved and put their foot down on things that will affect the personal lives of their employees. The event might trigger a series of unfortunate circumstances that will impact the employee's performance negatively.

The goal of team building is to improve the performance of the members of the team—if the event ends up causing personal issues that make them perform poorly, then the activity has failed to achieve its goal. In fact, it did the exact opposite. So, be wary of how the event affects the members on that aspect.

Additionally, team build activities aim to encourage camaraderie so there should be plenty of opportunity for the members to communicate and have fun. Sometimes, adding things that are not so wholesome causes more problems than if you had left them out. So, even though you are dealing with adults, try to keep things at GP level.

When organizing team games, make sure that the people participating are healthy enough to do the required physical activity for the games. If not, choose other team activities that will still accomplish the same goals, without pushing the members to their physical limits.

Remember, safety first.

30 Team Building Games

Chapter 6

Build a Nation

Number of Players: At least four

Materials: large sheets of white paper, pencils, crayons

In this game, divide the players into small groups (such as in pairs or small groups of at most ten members). Give each group the materials. Then, give the following instructions, "Your group has just arrived on an uninhabited island, and it is up to you to build it into a nation. Name your nation, design a flag, pick a national bird and flower, and compose your national anthem. The team must work together and then present their work in front.

Straw Tower

Number of Players: at least two

Materials: drinking straws, paper clips, pipe cleaners, string, scissors

In this team building activity, divide the players into two groups and provide them with the materials. Challenge each group to work together to build the highest possible tower without it toppling over. Give a time limit and declare a winner.

Paint Me a Picture

Number of Players: at least six
Materials: None

Before the start of the activity, write down at least five picture themes (such as "at a beach," or "riding the bus"). Then, divide the players into two or more groups. Tell them that you will call out a theme and they have to work together to depict it. Limit their time to prepare for the "picture." After the timer, they should not move while a judge evaluates their "picture."

Franken-stain

Number of Players: at least six

Materials: sheets of paper, a black marker, crayons, scotch tape

In this team building exercise, divide the players into two groups. The players should work together to form a complete silhouette of a body by tracing their different body parts and then sticking them together. Once the body is created, they should present their work.

Team Score

Number of Players: at least six
Materials: basketball, basketball court

Divide the players into two teams to play basketball using the regular rules. This time, though, a team can only win if every person is able to score no more than one point.

Story Building

Number of Players: at least three
Materials: None.

In this group activity, players form a circle and sit down comfortably on chairs or on the ground. The first player starts the story using only three sentences; he or she can introduce any character, setting, and plot. After three sentences, the player to his or her left should continue using three sentences, and so on. Have as many rounds as you like.

Walking Billboard

Number of Players: at least six

Materials: Sheets of thick paper, sticky tape, pens

Each player should write his or her name on the top of one sheet of paper. Then, the paper should be secured on their back with the tape. The players should then move around the room and write positive notes about the person whose name is on the paper. The game stops once everyone has written on everyone's paper.

Special Traits

Number of Players: at least six

Materials: paper, pencils

Instruct everyone to write his or her special traits on a sheet of paper. Then, tell them to look for traits in each player that are not the same as theirs. Give them a time limit. The player who has the longest list wins.

Sinking Boat

Number of Players: at least 10

Materials: two long pieces of ropes

Divide the players into two groups. Tie each long rope into a large loop, large enough to barely accommodate all the team members standing inside. Declare, "The boat is sinking, the boat is sinking. Who will you save?" Give them a time minute (such as five seconds), then make the loop smaller. The team has to find ways to keep everyone inside the loop.

Where is my match?

Number of Players: an even number of at least 10

Materials: pen, small pieces of paper, pen

Prepare a list of common pairs (such as salt and pepper, bread and butter, etc.). Write them down on the small sheets of paper, and then secretly tape them on the back of each player. Players have to ask each other yes or no questions to find out what is written on their back. Once they have found out, they should ask yes or no questions to find their partner.

Show Your Emotions

Number of Players: at least four

Materials: paper, pens

Before the game, write down at least five scenes (such as "at a park," "in the office," etc.). Divide the players into small groups of 2 to 6 members. Give each team a list of emotions (at least one per person) and the materials. Tell the players to work together to use the emotions in depicting the scene. Then, say the scene aloud and give them a time limit to depict it with the emotions. Have the teams depict the scene one at a time to allow the other team to guess the emotions and scene.

Egg Drop

Number of Players: at least four
Materials: eggs, newspapers, plastic wrap, straws, rubber bands, balloons, and other construction materials

Divide the players into small groups. Instruct each group to create a container that will protect an egg from breaking when dropped from a two-story building (or higher). Set a time limit for the construction. The team with the egg intact will win. If there is more than one team with eggs intact, the height could be increased little by little until only one or a few survives.

The Mummy

Number of Players: at least six

Materials: rolls of toilet paper

Divide the players into teams with at least three players per team. Instruct them to choose one player to be the mummy, and then give a time limit to wrap the player in toilet paper. The best mummy wins.

Team Cheer

Number of Players: at least six

Materials: None

Divide the players into two teams. Each team is given a time limit to come up with a cheer and dance routine. After which, each team should present their cheer in front of a judge. The most creative one wins.

Trip to the Market

Number of Players: at least six

Materials: None.

Divide the players into two teams. Have the first player say, "I went to the market to buy..." and then state something that starts with A (such as "apples,"), the second player continues by repeating the phrase, the item mentioned, and then include something that starts with B (such as "bread") and so on. The team whose members never missed an item wins.

Three Truths, One Lie

    Number of Players: at least six
    Materials: small sheets of paper, pens

Give four sheets to each player and instruct them to write three truths and one lie about themselves. Afterward, have each member read their truths and lies aloud at random. Let the others guess which one is the lie, and let the guessers explain why they think so.

Sell Me This Pen

    Number of Players: at least four
    Materials: a collection of office supplies

This is one of the team building activities for work. Divide the players into small teams. Give each team an office item and tell them they need to sell it. There must be a marketing plan, a logo, a slogan, and so on. Give a time limit for preparation, and then have them present their "product."

Newspaper Dance

Number of Players: at least six

Materials: sheets of old newspaper

In this team game, divide the players into small teams (two to four members each). Give them a sheet of newspaper and tell them to have everyone step on it when the music stops. Play the music, then stop and let them step on the newspaper without anyone's feet on the bare ground. Then, let them fold the paper in half and play the music again. Players must work together to stay on the newspaper as it is continuously folded into a smaller piece.

Turn the Sheet

Number of Players: at least four

Material: sheets of paper, each with X written on one side.

Divide the players into pairs. Let each pair stand on one sheet of paper, X side facing down. Then, ask everyone to turn over his or her sheet to reveal the X without stepping off it.

Rescue Mission

Number of Players: at least six

Materials: collection of office supplies

Divide the players into two teams. Tell the teams that each member should choose one office item they think would help them in an emergency. Give them a rescue mission (the house is on fire and you need to save a little girl inside). Then, let them elaborate on how they can work together to use their office items during the rescue.

Secret Code

Number of Players: at least three

Materials: None

Choose on player to leave the room so as not to hear the others. Tell the rest to choose a secret word. When the player returns, everyone must converse with him or her until he or she can say the secret word without him or her hinting it. They can only ask questions and get the person to talk. Once they have guessed it, another player is chosen to leave the room.

Pigs Fly

Number of Players: at least three
Materials: None

Choose an "It." Everyone then forms a circle around the It, who should call out, "ducks fly," "eagles fly," "bees fly," and so on. After mentioning each, the others should flap their arms as if flying. When the It says, "pigs fly" or some other animal that does not, no one should flap their arms. The person who does becomes the next It.

Mystery Item

Number of Players: at least four
Materials: None

In this team building game, choose two players to secretly choose an item in the room. Have them talk about the secret item without saying the name directly. Let everyone else listen and guess what it is.

Trash to Treasure

Number of Players: at least four
Materials: scissors, glue, tape, assorted recyclable items such as newspaper, egg cartons, paper towels, and so on

Divide the players into small teams and instruct them to create art out of the items on the pile. They must have an interesting story and name for their art, which they will explain after its construction.

The Human Spring

Number of Players: at least six
Materials: None

Divide the players into pairs. Have each pair face each other, then let Partner A turn around so that their back faces Partner B. Have Partner B hold out their arms. Tell Partner A to fall freely to let Partner B catch them. Vice versa.

The Line-up

Number of Players: at least 10
Materials: None

Divide the players into teams with at least three players per team. Instruct them to line up according to order based on the characteristic called out. After calling out a characteristic (such as age, birthday, height, weight, number of boyfriends or girlfriends, etc.), give them a time limit to work together.

Likes and Dislikes

Number of Players: at least six
Materials: small sheets of paper, pens

In this icebreaker, have everyone write down five likes and five dislikes on a sheet of paper. Collect the cards, read one like or dislike and have everyone guess the person to whom it belongs.

Sounds and Feelings

Number of Players: at least two
Materials: sound player, recording of different sounds, pens, paper

Give each member a pen and some paper. Then, instruct them to write the first emotion or memory that comes to mind for each sound you will play. After playing the sounds, have the members share what they wrote down.

Minefield

Number of Players: at least four
Materials: common office supplies

In an empty room, scatter the office supplies with just enough space between them for a person to pass through. Do not let the players see the room yet. Divide the players into groups, and then have one blindfolded and guided into the room. The team members should stand on the other end of the room and give instructions to keep the blindfolded player from stepping on the "mines" until they reach their team members.

Blind Artist

Number of Players: at least four

Materials: paper, pens

In this group activity, divide the players into pairs and have them sit with their backs against each other. The first player is given an object and the second player a pen and paper. The first player has to describe the picture without saying what it is to let the second player sketch it.

Evaluation of Results

Chapter 7

Each team building activity should be properly documented. When we say properly documented, it means that from planning to conclusion, including personal observations, should be well documented. There are two reasons for documentation of team building activities:

1. To create progressive team building activities in the future

2. To use it as a gauge for assessing the direction of the team and how to reach their goal more quickly and more efficiently.

Basing the info on the results of the activity will give you a clear cut idea of the kind of people you are working with. From there, you can plan the next activities, making sure to hit other target areas you need to address.

Remember, to not plan to address *all* the problem areas of your team. Do it progressively, and try to address the most pertinent problem first. To find out what is the first issue you should address, ask yourself which one will impede your team's performance? Is it the connection? Is it the motivation? Is it a trust issue? Is it personality friction? Or is insubordination?

Whatever it is, if it's the reason why the team won't move forward, address it first and move onto the next issues on your next team building activity.

By knowing what to address, you can customize your team building games to solve one of the issues, until you have addressed all of them and nothing more need to be tackled. Then, concentrate on just building the relationship of your team.

Finally, make sure that after every team building activity, you and your members will be able to look back and feel joy. The idea is to build, and in order to build the team, the team should feel happy while doing these activities. If they enjoyed this activity, they will look forward to the next.

Before you go + FREE BOOK

Thank you again for reading this book!

If you want to become more productive and get more done. The you can get a free copy of our productivity book.

Just head over to www.mindplans.com and you will find the free productivity book there.

I hope this book was able to help you to organize team building activities soon. I hope that it has also given ideas on how to make your own team games. Team building is important and it is not just about having parties, though they are usually fun.

Team build activities serve a purpose in developing the members and it has an impact on the company as a whole.

So, I hope that you have gotten all the information you need to start on your first team build! Hope you have incredible fun and hope your team learns teamwork!

The next step is to apply all that you have learned from this book.

Finally, if you enjoyed this book, then I'd like to ask you for a favor, would you be kind enough to leave a review for this book on Amazon? It'd be greatly appreciated!

Thank you and good luck!

♥ **Copyright 2016 by Mindplans - All rights reserved.**

This document is geared towards providing exact and reliable information in regards to the topic and issue covered. The publication is sold with the idea that the publisher is not required to render accounting, officially permitted, or otherwise, qualified services. If advice is necessary, legal or professional, a practiced individual in the profession should be ordered.

- From a Declaration of Principles which was accepted and approved equally by a Committee of the American Bar Association and a Committee of Publishers and Associations.

In no way is it legal to reproduce, duplicate, or transmit any part of this document in either electronic means or in printed format. Recording of this publication is strictly prohibited and any storage of this document is not allowed unless with written permission from the publisher. All rights reserved.

The information provided herein is stated to be truthful and consistent, in that any liability, in terms of inattention or otherwise, by any usage or abuse of any policies, processes, or directions contained within is the solitary and utter responsibility of the recipient reader. Under no circumstances will any legal responsibility or blame be held against the publisher for any reparation, damages, or monetary loss due to the information herein, either directly or indirectly.

Respective authors own all copyrights not held by the publisher.

The information herein is offered for informational purposes solely, and is universal as so. The presentation of the information is without contract or any type of guarantee assurance.

The trademarks that are used are without any consent, and the publication of the trademark is without permission or backing by the trademark owner. All trademarks and brands within this book are for clarifying purposes only and are the owned by the owners themselves, not affiliated with this document.

www.ingramcontent.com/pod-product-compliance
Lightning Source LLC
Chambersburg PA
CBHW070419190526
45169CB00003B/1332